Just Be*TWEEN* Us

A 31-day Devotional for Tweens

Shari A. Loveday

Just Between Us

ISBN 978-1-7349844-1-5

Dedication

I dedicate this book to all the little ladies who question their worth and to the ones who don't. Be kind to each other, cuz we're all just figuring it out as we go.

Table of Contents

Author's Note

I wrote this book because I wish someone would have told me God's heart for me when I was young. I went through life looking for love in all the wrong places. I didn't know that God wanted to be a part of every area of my life, that He knew things about me that no one else knew, and still loved me. I didn't know I could tell Him my deep, down secrets and that He had things He wanted to tell me. I wrote so that you would know all the good things God has planned for you, how much He loves you, and that the Bible is His love letter to you. The "Hey Baby Girl" section is God talking directly to you from the love letters he left for you in the Bible. The devotional thought follows the love letter and shares more about what it could mean. God may speak to you differently from the same text. That is what is so miraculous about his love letters. Somehow, they are tailored made for you... and me... and her... and them. Have a pen or pencil nearby so that you can journal the thoughts that come out of the "Think About It" section. Then, to complete your moment with God, you get to talk to him. You can use the prayer at the end of each devotion or speak to him in your own words. Whatever you do, keep the conversation going. Maybe, you will read one devotional over a week and choose to do each part day by day. Whichever way you decide to read it, *just between us*, I hope you fall in love with God as you read because He sure is in love with you and His love has the power to change your whole life.

Shari

HEY BABY GIRL,

Don't copy the behavior and customs of this world, but let God transform you into a new person by changing the way you think. Then you will learn to know God's will for you, which is good and pleasing and perfect. Romans 12:2

YOU NEED A FACTORY RESET

You've been listening to all the wrong people. Anyone that tells you negative things about you is a hater. I'm not talking about family and friends highlighting areas where you can grow. No, I'm talking about *frenemies* that say things like, "Why do you wear your hair like that. It's not cute." The things you've heard make it so you don't even know you are beautiful, smart, worthy, ready, and rare. Don't let the hateful criticisms of others leave you feeling unlovable. I made you well, and I love you very much. Just like with your cellphone, mean words and actions can be like a virus that messes with the way your mind works. A factory reset erases viruses and returns the phone to the original way it was made. It is time for a factory reset. I can set you free from thoughts that hold you back. Let me give you the factory reset you need.

THINK ABOUT IT

What negative things do you say to yourself? Write them out. Then rip the paper to shreds. That is the beginning of the end of you being negative about you.

I did this and it made me feel better.

Write 3 positive things or affirmations you can say to yourself?

I can say that I am, pretty, I have great hair, and that there is nothing wrong about me.

HEY GOD,

I've learned so many things over the years that have ruined my understanding of myself. I'm ready for you to reset my mind and give me a do-over. I want to have healthy thoughts about myself and about you. Help me read your love letters so that I'll make room for you to talk to me, begin to see myself the way you do, and talk to myself in more positive ways. Thanks in advance for my factory reset.

TTYL

When Jesus woke up, he rebuked the wind and said to the waves, "Silence! Be still!" Suddenly the wind stopped, and there was a great calm. Then he asked them, "Why are you afraid? Do you still have no faith?" Mark 4:38-40

YOU ARE OKAY

I know it seems like I don't care when your life feels like a storm, but I am using the storm. I'm using your challenges to make you a better you. I know you might be tempted to believe that I've forgotten about you, I'm not paying attention to you, or that I don't care, but that isn't true. When nothing seems to be going right, I'm here. When you face challenges, I'm here. I have never left you or turned away from you. At the right moment, I'll quiet the storms in your life. I need you to hold on and believe that I'm working to make you phenomenal despite all you've been through. The challenges in your life are mine to deal with. Trust that I never take my eyes off you and that I'm working everything out for your good. You're okay. I am with you.

THINK ABOUT IT

What challenges are you facing right now?

_____

_____

_____

_____

What are some of your strengths?

_____

_____

_____

_____

In what ways do you think I could be using your challenges to make a masterpiece out of you?

_____

_____

_____

_____

HEY GOD,

I'm tired and scared that my life will always be just a string of challenges. I can't see my way out. I don't know if I'm ever going to feel your *Son*light on my face again. Please hold me and help me feel your love. Help me believe that you have not left me, that you don't waste anything, and that you're using the storm to make me better. I trust you. Help me trust you more. Thanks in advance for helping my trust get bigger than my doubt and for helping me know I am going to be okay.

TTYL

HEY BABY GIRL,

Thank you for making me so wonderfully complex! Your workmanship is marvelous—how well I know it. Psalm 139:14

YOU ARE BEAUTIFUL

Do you have any idea how beautiful you are? I made you in the most intricate and intentional way. Your nose, your hair, your ears, your lips, all beautiful by my design. I have even placed beautiful things inside you. Your character and personality, both beautiful parts of you. Do you worry because it doesn't seem others think you are beautiful? Are you concerned because the media's idea of beauty looks nothing like you? Well, I was despised too. No one regarded me as special, but I was literally God, covered in human skin. Sometimes, humans miss the beauty of a person because they are looking for the wrong thing. Don't worry if others can't see your beauty. Those who are meant to, will. But even if they never do, know that I think you are to die for!

What causes you to question your beauty?

_____

_____

_____

_____

What are some ways you can help yourself believe in your own beauty?

_____

_____

_____

_____

Write 3 things you think are beautiful about you.

_____

_____

_____

_____

HEY GOD,

I worry about what others think of me so much that I try to change myself sometimes. I don't always believe I'm beautiful because the world's standard of beauty doesn't often look like me. I believe that the way you made me is wonderful. I don't think you made any mistakes. Thanks in advance for helping me see and believe in my own beauty.

TTYL

"It is like a person building a house who digs deep and lays the foundation on solid rock. When the floodwaters rise and break against that house, it stands firm because it is well built." Luke 6:48

YOU ARE UNBREAKABLE

I know you want to have a good life. You look at friends and crushes and you want to spend all your time with them. You want to tell them your hopes and dreams. You want them to love you. When the relationship doesn't work out, you feel shattered. You feel this way because you've built your life on humans who change their minds. You've buried your secrets in treasure chests that rot and decay. Instead, I'm asking you to trust in Me because I don't change my mind. Bring your funny stories, your hurts, your hopes, dreams, and secrets to me. You can confidently build your life on me, knowing I will never walk away from you or share your secrets with anyone. I am offering you the most stable relationship you will ever have. Build your life on Me, and you will always be unbreakable.

THINK ABOUT IT

Who or what have you built your life on?

_____

_____

_____

_____

Think about what it will look like to carefully begin to build your life on Me.

_____

_____

_____

_____

What will you need to do differently?

_____

_____

_____

_____

I want to build my life on you. I need a love that doesn't go away no matter what. Help me to feel your love like ocean waves washing over me. My trust has been broken by others, and I'm not sure I can trust again. I don't know how to be in a relationship with you, but you can show me how. My heart is yours. Thanks in advance for helping me build my life on you so I'll always be unbreakable.

TTYL

HEY BABY GIRL,

"Have I not commanded you? Be strong and courageous. Do not be afraid; do not be discouraged, for the Lord your God will be with you wherever you go." Joshua 1:9

YOU ARE STRONG

You are strong. I know sometimes you think you aren't, but I've seen your strength. I have watched you decide to survive no matter how hard things have gotten. Strength is the capacity of an object or substance to withstand great force or pressure. You've survived all the pressures beautifully. I wouldn't allow a challenge into your life if I thought it was going to break you. No, I know your strength intimately because I gave it to you, and I am using the pressures of your life to refine you. Think about diamonds. They can't become the beautiful things they are unless pressure is applied. The enemy is using pressure to try to crush you, but I'm using it to make something even more brilliant out of you.

THINK ABOUT IT

What causes you to feel strong?

_____

_____

_____

_____

What causes you to feel weak?

_____

_____

_____

_____

How can leaning on me when you are weak, make my strength perfect in you?

_____

_____

_____

_____

HEY GOD,

I don't always feel strong. When I cry or feel hurt by something, I feel weak. Please help me remember that showing emotion doesn't make me weak and that when I feel discouraged or fearful, I can lean on your strength. Thanks in advance for helping me see the strength I have and for making me stronger.

TTYL

For God has not given us a spirit of fear and timidity, but of power, love, and self-discipline. 2 Timothy 1:7

YOU ARE NOT BUGGIN' OUT

When I made you, I did not include fear in your DNA. I haven't given you that. I made you with love, peace, and a healthy mind, but you aren't buggin' out. You do experience things that cause you to feel fear and anxiety. When you experience fear, it is the enemy trying to make you anxious and take away your peace. If you'll trust in me, you'll have peace of mind. You will know that even though things look or feel difficult, all will be well because I am in control. When anxiety tries to tell you that you should spend time and energy worrying about things you can't control or things that haven't happened yet, tell your anxiety that your God didn't make you to worry about things He *can* control.

18

THINK ABOUT IT

What do you worry about?

_____
_____
_____
_____

Do you trust me? Is there anything in your life
you don't trust me with?

_____
_____
_____
_____

HEY GOD,

I want to trust you with my life so that anxiety
won't take over. I'm tired of worrying about
things I can't control. Please help me to leave
my problems and concerns in your hands,
believing that you're the one in control of my life.
Thanks in advance for helping me trust you
more and for giving me peace.

TTYL

So be strong and courageous! Do not be afraid and do not panic before them. For the LORD your God will personally go ahead of you. He will neither fail you nor abandon you." Deuteronomy 31:6

YOU ARE COURAGEOUS

You think that because you are afraid that means you are not courageous, but courage cannot exist without fear. Courage is not the absence of fear, my sweet, but it is facing your fears. I can hear you thinking, *why would I face something I am afraid of?* Because I am with you. You can face your fears because you know you are on the winning team. I have your back. You can do anything I've called you to do because I am fighting for you. When I went to the cross, I finished the fight! My blood made it so you win! All you have to do is claim your victory. You are more courageous than you know. Will you face your fears with me?

What scares you?

_____

_____

_____

_____

To whom do you go when you feel scared?

_____

_____

_____

_____

Here are some Bible texts you can memorize that will help you be courageous when you are afraid?

Deuteronomy 31:6

2 Timothy 1:7

Matthew 28:20

Hebrews 13:5

HEY GOD,

I want to be courageous, but sometimes I feel so frightened by some of the things that are happening in my life. Help me to believe that with you on my side, I win and I don't have anything to fear. Thanks in advance for increasing my courage.

TTYL

For the Lord gives wisdom; from his mouth come knowledge and understanding. Proverbs 2:6

YOU ARE SMART

I know you wonder about your intelligence when you have a difficult class or a teacher whose educational style does not complement your learning style, or when your learning challenges present you with barriers you don't know how to surmount. You wonder why your friends seem to have it so much easier than you in certain subjects. I want you to know that you are smart. The way you fight through your challenges and find ways to excel, that takes brilliance, and I made you to shine like that. You are made in a complex way that not even you may understand just yet, but I will help you understand yourself and your capabilities. I will help you excel.

What subjects challenge you? Surrender them to me and I will help you do your very best.

_____

_____

_____

_____

In what ways do people misunderstand you sometimes?

_____

_____

_____

_____

Has anyone ever caused you to wonder about how smart you are?

_____

_____

_____

_____

HEY GOD,

The world causes me to think I have to know it all and if I don't, I'm not smart, but I believe what you say about me. I believe I am smart because you made me in your image, with intentionality and creativity. Thanks in advance for helping me do my best, reach my full potential, and believe I'm smart.

TTYL

"Tune your ears to wisdom, and concentrate on understanding. Proverbs 2:2

YOU ARE WISE

You can't find wisdom in a book. Oh, wait, you actually can. My book. I will give you wisdom when you talk with me and listen to me. I will fill you with truth that you could not otherwise know or understand. It won't just be random facts. The things I share with you will be the links to a life you'll love. I'll help you choose the people you'll spend your life with and the work you'll devote yourself to. I will help you see what is most important in life. I know you think your friends, teachers, and parents are wise. They are, but no one is as wise as I am. If you ask, I will give you wisdom just like I did for Solomon. This will help you live the best possible life.

What foolish choices have you made recently?

_____

_____

_____

_____

What do you think I would have told you to do if you had asked me for wisdom?

_____

_____

_____

_____

HEY GOD,

I don't always make the best choices.

Sometimes, I do things to be cool or accepted even though I know it isn't a good idea. Please help me to view wisdom from you as the answer for how to live a good life. Thanks in advance for helping me seek wisdom from you.

TTYL

HEY BABY GIRL,

People can tame all kinds of animals, birds, reptiles, and fish, but no one can tame the tongue. It is restless and evil, full of deadly poison. James 3:7

YOU ARE KIND

Sometimes people around you behave in unkind ways. Your friends may talk badly about another kid, say something snarky to someone else's face, or post a negative comment on social media to make someone feel small. Deep in your heart, you know none of those things are okay to say to someone. You would never want someone to talk to you like that. I made you to be kind and sweet to others. That uncomfortable feeling you get when someone is being unkind is a compass leading you back to kindness. What you say matters. You have the power to build someone up or tear them down. I made you to build others up. I made you kind.

Have you ever treated someone unkindly?

_____

_____

_____

_____

Have you ever been treated unkindly? How did
you feel?

_____

_____

_____

_____

What do you think the Bible means when it says
we can tame animals but not our tongues?

_____

_____

_____

_____

HEY GOD,

I want to be kind. I believe you made me that way. Sometimes, I'm not kind to others or I don't speak up when others are being mean. Please help me to be who you made me to be. Fill me with your Holy Spirit so that I will show the fruit of the Spirit. Thanks in advance for helping me be as kind as you made me to be.

TTYL

HEY BABY GIRL,

Oh, the joys of those who do not follow the advice of the wicked, or stand around with sinners, or join in with mockers. Psalm 1:1

YOU DESERVE THE BEST

You are so special. You deserve the best. Don't settle for friends or crushes that don't see your value. You will come across people who want to be with you for different reasons. Some will want stuff from you, some will want your influence so they can be popular, and some will want to take precious pieces of you to fulfill their own desires. Don't let someone lead you down a path that pulls you out of my will for your life. Set a boundary around yourself that accepts nothing but the very best. There are people who will see you for who you really are and be drawn to you. You don't have to settle for anything less. You deserve the best.

Do you believe you deserve the best?

_____

_____

_____

_____

Have you settled for less in a relationship with a friend or a crush?

_____

_____

_____

_____

What is one thing you can do to remind yourself and others that you deserve the best?

_____

_____

_____

_____

HEY GOD,

I don't always believe I deserve the best. Sometimes, I settle because I wonder if I am good enough, and I allow people to do things to me and around me that aren't right. I do it to please other people so they can like me, but it makes me feel bad about myself later. Please help me to set healthy boundaries around myself. Help me see when someone loves me and when they don't, when someone is taking me off course, or when someone is not good for me. Thanks in advance for helping me choose the best for myself.

TTYL

For I know the plans I have for you," says the LORD. "They are plans for good and not for disaster, to give you a future and a hope. In those days when you pray, I will listen. If you look for me wholeheartedly, you will find me. Jeremiah 29:11-13

YOU ARE A DREAMER

I know you have dreams. I placed them inside your heart. I placed your gifts inside you too. I know what causes you to feel happy and excited. Your dreams are not too big for me. I can't wait to help make them come true. I'm working for you while you dream. You have a part to play, but sometimes you come face to face with barriers that get in your way. The impossibility is what makes it a dream. Don't give up. Soon, you will see my hand in your dreams. Don't you remember Joseph? I gave him his dreams and just when it seemed like he couldn't be farther away from them becoming a reality, *I* did it. I will do the same for you, so keep right on dreaming!

THINK ABOUT IT

What dreams have you dreamed? Write them down here or in your journal, on your vision board, or on a piece of paper. Give me your dreams, pray about them, and watch me work.

_____

_____

_____

_____

_____

HEY GOD,

Sometimes, I think my dreams are pointless. I wonder if they'll ever come true because some of them sound so silly. It has been hard to believe in my dreams when others don't. Now I know my dreams were placed in my heart by you. Help me to be on the same page with you about the when and how of my dreams. Thanks in advance for making my dreams a reality.

TTYL

Then the angry king sent the man to prison to be tortured until he had paid his entire debt. "That's what my heavenly Father will do to you if you refuse to forgive your brothers and sisters from your heart."
Matthew 18:34-35

YOU ARE FORGIVING

Has anyone ever lied about you or mistreated you? That has happened to me. When the very people I came to save put me up on the cross, I felt rejected and abused. When others have lied about, abandoned, or haven't loved you the way you need to be loved, I can show you what to do with your hurts. You've been carrying them like a heavy backpack filled with books you don't need. I will show you how to forgive. Forgiveness helps you put down the heavy baggage. It's my way of healing you. I want to help you feel better, but sometimes it seems you want to hold onto the things that hurt you deeply.

You think that holding on to what others have done will somehow make you strong against future hurts, but it just gets in the way of you experiencing love. Let me show you how forgiveness sets you free.

THINK ABOUT IT

In what ways have others hurt you?

_____

_____

_____

_____

What will you be able to do once those hurts are no longer holding you back?

_____

_____

_____

_____

HEY GOD,

Before I ask your forgiveness for the mistakes I've made, I'm asking you to help me forgive others. I've been able to let go of some things that have been holding me back, but I want to be free and healed from all of it. Please help me to give others the forgiveness you give me. Thanks in advance for helping me learn to forgive so I can be free.

TTYL

HEY BABY GIRL,

Whatever is good and perfect is a gift coming down to us from God our Father, who created all the lights in the heavens. He never changes or casts a shifting shadow. James 1:17

YOU ARE ADAPTABLE

How do you feel when things begin to change around you? Do you worry that the situation will become difficult for you? Do you worry that you will lose people or things that you love? Change can be hard, but I wanted to let you know that you can handle change because you love me and *I* never change. My feelings for you do not change. The love I have for you never goes away. I've made plans for you that are good. They will benefit you and help you have a good life. They do not shift based on what is happening today. I will be faithful, even in the middle of everything else changing in your life. I will do all that I've said. That promise is why you can handle change.

What is changing around you?

_____

_____

_____

_____

What do you fear will happen as a result of the change?

_____

_____

_____

_____

How can your trust in me and the plans I have for you help to calm your fears?

_____

_____

_____

_____

HEY GOD,

When change happens, sometimes I worry that I won't survive it. I wonder if the changes will ruin my life. Now I know that you do not change and that you have good plans for me, not to ruin me, but to make my life really good. Please help me remember that so I won't be afraid of change. Thanks in advance for helping me manage my thoughts and feelings about change.

TTYL

"If you fully obey the LORD your God and carefully keep all his commands that I am giving you today, the LORD your God will set you high above all the nations of the world. Deuteronomy 28:1

YOU ARE BLESSED

This world may give you the idea that your blessings are tied to where you live, what culture you're from, or how much money you have, but you should know that blessings are tied to me and only me. I bless you whether you are from the city or the country, whether you're slim or curvy, whether your hair is straight, kinky, or curly. My blessings don't work the way human favoritism does. I bless you in ways that will fulfill my plans for you. You are precious to me. I made you in my image, and I love you with everlasting love. Stop trying to change yourself to look like others so you can receive blessings. Just make the choice to be with me and you will find blessings in my presence.

THINK ABOUT IT

What are some of the things society says makes a person blessed?

_____

_____

_____

_____

What have you thought you were missing because you didn't look a certain way or own a particular thing?

_____

_____

_____

_____

Sometimes I feel like I'm not blessed because I don't have the hair or body or looks that seem to be what others think is best. I worry that I will never have popularity, fame or someone to love me because I don't look like people in magazines or on TV. Help me remember that I am special to you. I want to put my trust in your plan even if it doesn't lead to fame and fortune. Help me believe that your plan is good and tailor-made for me. Thanks in advance for blessing me.

TTYL

HEY BABY GIRL,

O LORD, you have examined my heart and know everything about me. You know when I sit down or stand up. You know my thoughts even when I'm far away. You see me when I travel and when I rest at home. You know everything I do. Psalm 139:1-3

YOU ARE KNOWN

There are times when you feel unknown by everyone around you. You have thoughts and feelings that go unheard, unfelt. You wonder if anyone really knows and understands you. I do. You are fully known by me. I capture your tears in a jar. Not one falls without my notice. I number the hairs on your head. I know when even just one comes out. You are funny and kind, sweet and sensitive. You are worried about things that no one else knows about. I know you well my darling child. I know the good things about you, the poor choices you make, the ugly thoughts you think, and I love you. I always will. Never forget. You are known and chosen by Me.

What makes you feel small and unknown?

_____
_____
_____
_____

What is something you love about yourself that many people don't see or know about?

_____
_____
_____
_____

Is it enough that I [God] know everything about you and I've chosen you to be mine?

_____
_____
_____
_____

HEY GOD,

I am so grateful that I'm known and loved by you. Sometimes, the way other people treat me makes me feel small. Sometimes, I feel like people just don't *see* me. I don't want to feel invisible or small, so please help me remember that the God who flung the stars and kissed the sun knows me, loves me, and has chosen me. Thanks in advance for helping me believe that being known by you is enough.

TTYL

"I know all the things you do, and I have opened a door for you that no one can close. You have little strength, yet you obeyed my word and did not deny me. Revelation 3:8

YOU ARE SEEN

I know sometimes you think no one truly sees you, but I do. I see who and how you are. I poured gifts into you that I can see working in your life. I see that your character is becoming sweeter and sweeter. Sometimes in this world, it looks like only certain types of people succeed, but I see you and I have opportunities for you that no one else can give you. When I begin to open doors for you, no one will be able to shut them. I will also have to close some doors because some will be a distraction the enemy will use to throw you off course. There are so many amazing plans I have for your future. I see you, and I am watching over

you to make sure all my good plans for you come
to be.

What do you want to be when you grow up?
Someone who helps people through a service
profession? Someone who invents new things?

_____
_____
_____
_____

What opportunities would you like to have
offered to you?

_____
_____
_____
_____

What opportunities might be a distraction for
you?

_____
_____
_____
_____

HEY GOD,

I'm so grateful that you see me. It's an awesome feeling to know that someone truly sees me for who I am. It's also great to know there are doors you plan to open and close to make my life good. Thanks in advance for the doors of opportunity you will open for me to live my blessed life.

TTYL

You saw me before I was born. Every day of my life was recorded in your book. Every moment was laid out before a single day had passed. Psalm 139:16

YOU ARE WHO I SAY YOU ARE

As you go through life, people will call you all kinds of things. Some will be positive and others not so much, but you must remember, you are who *I* say you are. I made you intentionally, never taking my eyes off your baking process. I put your personality in place. Your eye color was chosen by me. Your heart was forged in love by my own. Only I truly know who you were created to be because I did the work of creating you. Sure, your parents kicked in DNA, but guess who chose what you would get from each of them. When you are tempted to worry about some negative thing someone has said about you, pause and ask yourself, "Who knows me better than anyone, including me? What does God say about me?"

51

THINK ABOUT IT

What have people said about you that was positive? Negative?

_____

_____

_____

_____

Who do I say you are?

_____

_____

_____

_____

Find some positive things I have said about you in my word. Write them on sticky notes and stick them on your bedroom wall so you will remember the good things I have said about you. Start with some of the things you find in Psalm 139.

_____

_____

_____

_____

HEY GOD,

The things people say can hurt. I don't want to base how I feel about myself on what others say about me. I want to base it on what you say about me because I see now that you are the only one who actually knows the truth of who I am and who I will be. Help me remember all the sweet things you say about me. Thanks in advance for changing my view of myself to match what you think about me.

TTYL

This means that anyone who belongs to Christ has become a new person. The old life is gone; a new life has begun! 2 Corinthians 5:17

YOU ARE NEW

I know it is difficult for you to come to me after you've done something wrong. Sometimes, the guilt or shame you feel causes you to hide from me. Don't hide. I love you so much, and if you come to me, I can make you new. In fact, the moment you come and ask forgiveness, you are new. Try it now. Just ask, and you will be made a new creation, one without the sin of this world on you. It may not feel that way at first. You may still be holding onto what you've done. I desperately want to cover you with my goodness, but I can only do it if you come to me with your mistakes and your poor choices. I want to help you be the best you can be. You deserve a fresh start because I died so you could have it.

THINK ABOUT IT

Think about some of the poor choices you've made. Write them down in pencil and then color over them with a red marker until you can't see them anymore. This symbolizes what I've done for you. I have blotted out your sins just like you blotted out those words. How does it make you feel to know I've forgiven you?

_____

_____

_____

_____

_____

_____

_____

HEY GOD,

Help me remember that I don't have to hide my sins from you. Remind me to bring them to you so I can be made new. Thanks in advance for helping me leave guilt and shame behind so I can find my newness in you.

TTYL

But the Lord said to her, "My dear Martha, you are worried and upset over all these details! There is only one thing worth being concerned about. Mary has discovered it, and it will not be taken away from her."
Luke 10:38-42

YOU ARE THIS CLOSE

I've made a way for you to be saved, but I don't just want to save you. I want to *be* with you. I want to spend eternity with you, so I've made it so that you can be close to me right now. No one can get in the way. There is always space for you with me. You are this close. All you have to do is let me be with you. Let me into your heart. Talk with me when you wake up in the morning. Listen for me before you go to bed at night. Let my words be the first and last ones in your ear each day. Read the love letters I left for you. Sit in nature and find me in my creation. Nothing is more important than our relationship. Open your eyes and look around. You are this close.

THINK ABOUT IT

What causes you to feel close to me? What causes you to feel far from me?

_____

_____

_____

_____

HEY GOD,

A lot of the time, I feel like I'm far from you. I know that you are always close to me. Help me experience you and believe you are there even when I can't feel you. Help me want to read my Bible, talk to you, and listen to you more. Thanks in advance for helping me _know_ you're always close to me.

TTYL

The Lord kept his word and did for Sarah exactly what he had promised. She became pregnant, and she gave birth to a son for Abraham in his old age. This happened at just the time God had said it would. Genesis 21:1-2

YOU ARE PATIENT

Your whole life awaits. There are so many things you want to do. You want to fall in love, go to college, start a career. You want to see what your life is going to turn out like, but you can be patient. I've planned a beautiful life for you. My plans will exceed any expectation you have, but you will have to wait for it. See, waiting is a part of the process. While you wait, I will work everything out for your good. Don't ever think a moment is wasted because I do not waste anything! Every moment of your life is being used by me to make a miracle out of you.

What are you looking forward to in your future?

_____

_____

_____

_____

What are some things you've been waiting for?

_____

_____

_____

_____

Why do you think waiting is an essential part of your preparation for becoming who I made you to be?

_____

_____

_____

_____

I'm not so good at waiting. I get impatient, thinking that I will miss out on opportunities if it doesn't happen now. I hear you saying I am patient, that I can wait, and that what you are planning is worth the wait. Can you help me trust you with my life enough to be able to wait calmly? Thanks in advance for helping me to wait well.

TTYL

Three different times I begged the Lord to take it away. Each time he said, "My grace is all you need. My power works best in weakness." So now I am glad to boast about my weaknesses, so that the power of Christ can work through me.
2 Corinthians 12:8-9

YOU ARE GODFIDENT

When situations come up that you don't think you are ready for, when you are asked to do something you do not think you are capable of doing, when you feel like you are not enough, remember that my grace is enough. Because you have my power at your disposal, you can be *Godfident* that you are more than enough! You can walk into any room, knowing that you belong. You can sit at any table and offer your thoughts. You can sing, dance, play sports, and do presentations with full *Godfidence* because I am with you, and *I* am *more* than enough!

What causes you to feel confident?

_____

_____

_____

_____

What causes you to lose confidence?

_____

_____

_____

_____

HEY GOD,

I don't always feel confident, but I want to feel
that way wherever I go and in whatever I do.
Help me to remember that when I acknowledge
my limits and admit my weaknesses, that is
when your strength becomes more powerful in
me. Thanks in advance for giving me
Godfidence.

TTYL

HEY BABY GIRL,

If you listen to these commands of the Lord your God that I am giving you today, and if you carefully obey them, the Lord will make you the head and not the tail, and you will always be on top and never at the bottom. Deuteronomy 28:13

YOU ARE CRUSHIN' IT

I made you to crush it! That's right. When I decided to make you, I knew I was making someone who would be awesome, phenomenal, and special. Because of whose you are, you will do amazing things. I made you to be on top, never on the bottom. When you do not feel like you are at your best, those are the moments I use to hone your gifts. The truth is, you will crush it because you are my child. I will lead you to make the best choices. I will fill you with creativity. Excellence will be your only mode because that is how I made you. Apart from me, you cannot be successful, but your commitment to be with me will make crushin' it the only option.

THINK ABOUT IT

What tasks and goals are you wanting to do well?

_____

_____

_____

_____

Do you believe that being with me is the only way to have the very best life possible?

_____

_____

_____

_____

HEY GOD,

I don't always feel like I'm on top. Sometimes, I fail and that makes me feel like I am less than. Can you help me to remember that because I am your child, I am destined for excellence? Help me to believe I was made to crush it! When I fail, will you help me look at failure as a training ground for success? Thanks in advance for helping me crush it!

TTYL

But the Lord said to Samuel, "Don't judge by his appearance or height, for I have rejected him.
The Lord doesn't see things the way you see them.
People judge by outward appearance, but
the Lord looks at the heart." 1 Samuel 16:7

YOU ARE SUCCESSFUL

The world tries to set the standard for what success is. According to society, success is adults working high-powered corporate jobs and barely seeing their families, or superstars that get half-naked and shake it for all to see, or athletes that are really good at a game, or a Tik Tok sensation that breaks the internet. In this world, success is what you can see. In my kingdom, success is not that easy to see. It isn't in what you own or wear or post. Success is found in living out your purpose, no matter what it is. It is found in the closeness of your relationship with me. Success is in your character. Those are decisions that happen on the inside of your life, in the places no human eyes can go.

THINK ABOUT IT

What are some goals you set that you thought would make you successful because of the world's definition of success?

_____

_____

_____

_____

What do you think *I* want for you?

_____

_____

_____

_____

HEY GOD,

I got tricked into thinking that what people can see is what makes me successful. Please help me to remember that it is what's inside my heart and character that determine how successful I am. Thanks in advance for changing my mind about what success is.

TTYL

HEY BABY GIRL,

So you have not received a spirit that makes you fearful slaves. Instead, you received God's Spirit when he adopted you as his own children.
Romans 8:15

YOU ARE ADOPTED

I adopted you into my family even before you were made. You were born into the human family, but I've given you the opportunity to be a part of my heavenly family. You are now an heir to my kingdom. When I died for you, it wasn't so that I could make you a slave. No, I wanted to make you my child. Everything I have is yours because of this adoption. Being a part of my family comes with responsibility though. You must walk like me, talk like me, look like me. When people see you, they should see a family resemblance. The way you love others should introduce them to or remind them of me. Don't worry. I will help you with that part. All you have to do is open your heart to me.

How does it feel to know that you are my child?

_____
_____
_____
_____

In what ways do you resemble me?

_____
_____
_____
_____

In what ways would you like to look more like me?

_____
_____
_____
_____

70

HEY GOD,

I'm so grateful that you adopted me into your family. You gave up so much to make me your child. Help me never forget I've been adopted by you, that I can walk in the knowledge that you are my Dad, and talk like I'm an heiress. I want to remember that my life should remind others of you. Thanks in advance for helping me to adjust my crown and become more like you.

TTYL

A slave is not a permanent member of the family, but a son is part of the family forever. So if the Son sets you free, you are truly free. John 8:36

YOU ARE FREE

You are free from sin, free from what other people think of you, free from the law. Whoever I set free is really, truly free. You don't have to worry about the pressure of trying to make sure you don't break any rules. I will help you do that if you will just *be* with me. Don't worry about making poor or sinful choices. I will help you with that too. I will give you the strength to live like me supernaturally. That thought should make you free from the stress and pressure of being perfect, cuz guess what, no one is perfect. That is the big secret grown-ups in your life have been keeping. No one can be who I am calling them to be without *being* with me. Now you're free to just concentrate on your relationship with me.

THINK ABOUT IT

What have you been worrying about that you are now free from?

_____

_____

_____

_____

What will you do with your freedom?

_____

_____

_____

_____

HEY GOD,

I've felt so much pressure to do the right thing. In moments when I have not been able to do that, I've felt shame. Thank you for the freedom that you offer me to just focus on my relationship with you. That makes it so much easier to be your child. Thanks in advance for helping me stay free.

TTYL

For whoever finds me finds life and receives favor from the Lord. Proverbs 8:35

YOU ARE MY FAVORITE

You are my absolute favorite! I know you are wondering how that could be possible when I have so many other children. I am not like humans, limited to one favorite. I can favor you and not neglect another because I am God. If you understood how I did everything I do, I wouldn't be worthy of your worship. I want to bless you beyond any of your wildest hopes and dreams, but I have to take my time because you are still growing and changing. If I dropped all my favor on you at once, it would overwhelm you. I am intentional about how and when I bless you, but you must never doubt how I feel about you, even when you go through tough times. Never stop believing that you are my favorite.

THINK ABOUT IT

Take a moment and think about all the ways I've blessed you and your family.

_____

_____

_____

_____

Think about the tough times you've had. Ask yourself how I could be using those moments to give you the best life possible.

_____

_____

_____

_____

HEY GOD,

I didn't know I was your favorite. I don't know how you can favor me and your other children without one of us feeling left out, but I believe that you can. Help me to behave like I'm favored by you. Thanks in advance for all the blessings that are still to come.

TTYL

Love is patient and kind. Love is not jealous or boastful or proud or rude. It does not demand its own way. It is not irritable, and it keeps no record of being wronged. It does not rejoice about injustice but rejoices whenever the truth wins out. 1 Corinthians 13:4-6

YOU ARE LOVED

Do you know what love is? The best definition can be found in my love letter to you, 1 Corinthians 13. There, I tell you all about what love is. Others will try to teach you what love is from their perspective, but I am the best person to teach you about it because I didn't just invent love. I *am* love. I am kind and patient. I don't boast or get so filled with pride that I put myself before you. I am never rude or controlling. I forgive you as often as you ask. I never give up on you, even if you've given up on yourself. I am honest with you in ways that build you up, and never tear you down. Love is always good for you, never toxic. When someone doesn't love you, don't think there is anything wrong with you. Sometimes people are not capable of giving you what you need because of things they've never been given what they need. You can't offer what you don't have. When you look for people to share your life with, use my standard of love to choose.

THINK ABOUT IT

Think about moments when someone has said that they love you.

_____

_____

_____

_____

Now compare their behavior to my love letter in 1 Corinthians 13. Does it add up to love?

_____

_____

_____

_____

HEY GOD,

I want to know what love is. I want to know if someone really loves me. Please help me to use your love letter in 1 Corinthians 13 as my standard for love. Help me to see a counterfeit when it is being offered to me. When I find that someone doesn't love me, help me not to think something is wrong with me. Thanks in advance for letting your love set the standard in my life.

TTYL

HEY BABY GIRL,

"For this is how God loved the world: He gave his one and only Son, so that everyone who believes in him will not perish but have eternal life. John 3:16-17

YOU ARE LOVED II

You are loved. I mean with an earth-shattering, soul-shaking love. I gave you this gift. It won't cost you anything, though it cost me a everything. Thousands of years ago, I left heaven and all its glory to love you. I traded angelic adoration for the worship of poor shepherds. I left my Father's direct presence to be Emmanuel, God with you. I gave up the perfect home for Nazareth, all because I love you. My love can change everything in your life if you let it in. It will make sad moments purposeful. It will be a light in dark times. It will help you understand when you are confused. It will help you feel comforted when your friends are nowhere to be found. It will give you courage when you're afraid. It can fill you up to overflowing if you let it.

When have you felt unloved?

_____

_____

_____

_____

What in John 3:16-17 signals that I love you?

_____

_____

_____

_____

How could knowing you are loved make you ready for success?

_____

_____

_____

_____

HEY GOD,

Thank you for loving me. You loved me enough
to die for me! I needed to hear that today. Help
me remember that, especially in moments when
I feel alone or unloved. I want that thought to be
the thing that helps me keep it together when I
feel like falling apart. Thanks in advance for
always loving me.

TTYL

I heard a loud shout from the throne, saying, "Look, God's home is now among his people! He will live with them, and they will be his people. God himself will be with them. Revelation 21:3

YOU ARE LOVED III

This one is so important that I couldn't tell you just once. You are loved! I have so much love for you that I didn't just come and be God with you once, but I'm coming again. When I get back, I will cleanse the world of all that is wrong and bring a little heaven right down here on earth. I used to visit Adam and Eve in the garden of Eden, but I am going to *live* in the city I am making for you. You won't need lights or electricity. I will be the only light you need. I am making the new earth so special for you, but the best part is that we will always be together. There will never be a separation between you and me again. I love you that much!

THINK ABOUT IT

What are you looking forward to the most when you think about eternity with me?

_____

_____

_____

_____

How can we start our eternity together right now?

_____

_____

_____

_____

HEY GOD,

Some days, I don't feel loved. I'm so excited that you are making a place for me to be with you forever. Please help me to begin spending time with you so we can start eternity today. Thanks in advance for saving me a spot right next to you in the new earth and for loving me forever.

TTYL

I will make you my wife forever, showing you righteousness and justice, unfailing love and compassion. I will be faithful to you and make you mine, and you will finally know me as the Lord.
Hosea 2:19-20

YOU ARE MINE

You. Are. Mine. I will never give up on loving you. I will go to the ends of the earth to be with you. Even when you walk away from me, when you turn your back on our relationship, I will never stop loving you. I won't just sit passively by and wait for you. I will pursue you like someone who has lost a precious jewel that cost more than everything they own. You mean too much to me for me to ever stop chasing you. You will always be my heart's desire. I thought you were to die for, so I did it. I died for you. And I would do it again just to prove that you are mine. Will you offer me your yes today? Will you make the decision to be mine forever?

THINK ABOUT IT

Write a list of things that might be in the way of your relationship with me.

_____

_____

_____

_____

Next to each item on your list, write "worth it" or "not worth it" to decide if anything on your list is worth not being with me forever when I come back to take you home.

_____

_____

_____

_____

HEY GOD,

I love you so much! I am yours. Please help me to make you mine every day. I get off track and I forget about you, but I want you to be the most important person in my life. Thanks in advance for never giving up on me and for chasing me.

TTYL

I love seeing people get free of the things holding them back, and I have a special place in my heart for young women because I remember what it was like to struggle with low self-worth and question if I was lovable. I want young women coming up behind me to know that they are loved and worthy. I offer inspiration and therapy for that reason. To learn more about my ministry, check out LoveWellFamilyTherapy.com or follow me on IG @Lovewellfamilytherapy

Made in the USA
Columbia, SC
13 February 2022